111 Trees

How One Village Celebrates the Birth of Every Girl

Rina Singh
Marianne Ferrer

CitizenKid™

A collection of books that inform
children about the world and inspire
them to be better global citizens

Kids Can Press

This one is for Julian, Ethan, Quentin
and Auden — the future eco-feminists — R.S.

For you, the light that makes everything grow — M.F.

CitizenKid™ is a trademark of Kids Can Press Ltd.

Text © 2020 Rina Singh
Illustrations © 2020 Marianne Ferrer

Published in Canada and the U.S. by Kids Can Press Ltd.
25 Dockside Drive, Toronto, ON M5A 0B5

Kids Can Press is a Corus Entertainment Inc. company

www.kidscanpress.com

The artwork in this book was rendered in watercolor, gouache and graphite.
The text is set in Colby.

All photos courtesy of Rina Singh.

Edited by Jennifer Stokes
Designed by Marie Bartholomew

Printed and bound in Buji, Shenzhen, China, in 11/2021 by WKT Company

MIX
Packaging from
responsible sources
FSC® C010256

CM 20 0 9 8 7 6 5 4 3

Library and Archives Canada Cataloguing in Publication

Title: 111 trees : how one village celebrates the birth of every girl / Rina Singh ; Marianne Ferrer.
Other titles: One hundred and eleven trees
Names: Singh, Rina, 1955- author. | Ferrer, Marianne, 1990- illustrator.
Series: CitizenKid.
Description: Series statement: CitizenKid
Identifiers: Canadiana 20190215852 | ISBN 9781525301209 (hardcover)
Subjects: LCSH: Sex discrimination against women — India — Juvenile literature.
| LCSH: Sex discrimination against women — India — Prevention — Juvenile literature.
| LCSH: Women's rights — India — Juvenile literature. | LCSH: Equality — Juvenile literature.
| LCSH: Feminism — Juvenile literature.
Classification: LCC HQ1237.5.I4 S56 2020 | DDC j305.420954 — dc23

Kids Can Press gratefully acknowledges that the land on which our office is located
is the traditional territory of many nations, including the Mississaugas of the Credit,
the Anishnabeg, the Chippewa, the Haudenosaunee and the Wendat peoples,
and is now home to many diverse First Nations, Inuit and Métis peoples.

We thank the Government of Ontario, through Ontario Creates; the Ontario
Arts Council; the Canada Council for the Arts; and the Government of Canada
for supporting our publishing activity.

Preface

Not too long ago, a village in India was ruled by
ancient customs. There, the birth of a boy was celebrated
with the beating of pots and pans and the sharing
of sweets. A son was a blessing from the gods,
someone who would carry on the family name
and take care of aging parents.

The birth of a girl was welcomed with silence.
A daughter was a burden, someone who would cost parents
a dowry (money given to the groom's family) when she got
married and who would become the property of her husband.

But today, things are different in that village.
Today, 1 girl = 111 trees.
This story is true, and it started with a boy named Sundar.

Sundar watches how his mother balances the water pot on her head. Walking to the well with her every day in the blistering heat is hard, but it's his favorite thing to do. It's the only time he has her all to himself. On the way back, they stop under some trees, and she asks him to collect pieces of firewood for cooking.

He sees her smile at him through her veil.

At night, Sundar feels his mother's wet cheeks as she hushes him and his two hungry sisters to sleep.

Their mud house is too small for his family of eleven.

One night, Sundar's mother
is bitten by a poisonous snake.
In the morning, she doesn't
wake up. The villagers come to
the door, wail loudly and take
her away. And just like that,
his mother is gone.

After this, whenever Sundar sees women walking to the well, he runs to wrap his arms around a tree, pretending to hug his mother.

Years pass.

Sundar grows up, marries and becomes a father. He has two daughters and a son, and he and his wife raise them with equal love and joy.

As his children grow, he teaches them the names of trees and birds.

He shows them how their lives depend on the natural world.

He guides them to embrace all forms of life.

Sundar works as a laborer in a marble factory not far from his village. The process of mining the marble strips the soil, dumps waste into the land and leaves the landscape dry and barren, making any kind of farming difficult.

He asks the factory owners to plant trees to make up for the harm they are doing to the countryside, but they refuse. Sundar begins to fear for the future well-being of his village. He is so angry that he leaves his job.

Sundar brims with ideas to make life better for the people of his village. He wants no one to live in fear of hunger. He wants all children — boys *and* girls — to go to school and not spend their childhoods working the fields or fetching water. He wants to heal the land ravaged by irresponsible mining. He dreams of planting trees.

He runs in the election to become *sarpanch*, the village head, and he wins.

One year later, his older daughter dies after a brief illness. Sundar is heartbroken. He shuts himself in a room and cries for twelve days. On the thirteenth day, he comes out and plants some saplings, burying his grief into the earth.

Sundar imagines the saplings growing into magnificent trees that will live for hundreds of years. And with them will live the memory of his daughter.

All of a sudden, Sundar knows what he has to do.

Every GIRL

born in the village will be welcomed with the planting of

111 trees.

Sundar shares his idea with the men and women of the village. The villagers think Sundar has lost his mind. They reject his plan. It's against their tradition to honor girls. They argue. They are afraid the world will laugh at them. They don't understand this new way of thinking.

But Sundar keeps talking to the villagers. He shows them
how the factory is slowly destroying the land. He tells them
of other nations where girls and boys are treated equally,
where there is plenty of water and electricity and enough
wealth and knowledge to go to the moon. He even offers to
plant the trees in the girls' names himself — *if* the villagers
promise to send their daughters to school and wait to marry
them off until they turn eighteen.

Slowly, very slowly, the villagers begin to understand that by welcoming girls and planting trees, they might bring balance back to nature.

They worry about the water the trees will need, but Sundar has a plan for that, too. He brings in engineers from the city, and the villagers learn how to harvest rain by digging trenches to store water — water that can also be used for drinking. When termites infect some of the trees, the women grow aloe vera plants to cure them.

Soon, the men see that women no longer have to walk for hours to fetch water. The women see that their children are no longer hungry. The trees are making life better for everyone. The villagers begin to place their trust in Sundar. And every time a girl is born, the villagers plant 111 trees.

The trees and the girls grow up together. Mothers and daughters take care of the trees. At the end of every summer, girls tie sacred threads around the trunks to renew their bonds with them.

The village prospers, and the trees continue to grow.
Today, mango, papaya, neem, sheesham and amla
trees line the roads and cascade down the hillsides.

There is enough water
for everyone in the village.
Girls go to school and
learn along with the boys.
And to this day, every
time 1 girl is born, 111 trees
are planted.

More about Sundar and Piplantri

Shyam Sundar Paliwal loves trees. If you meet him and ask to take his photo, he will quickly wrap his arms around the nearest one.

Piplantri is a small village in the desert state of Rajasthan, India. When Sundar was elected as its *sarpanch*, or village head, Piplantri was dusty and had been deforested by Asia's largest marble industry. Having once worked in the marble mines, Sundar knew firsthand how mining for marble was hurting the countryside. As *sarpanch*, he hoped to find a way to heal the land.

One year after being elected, Sundar lost his older daughter, Kiran, to dehydration. While mourning for her, he came up with the idea of celebrating her life by planting trees in her memory.

And then he had another idea:

Why just my daughter?

Why not *all* daughters?

Sundar Paliwal surrounded by trees

Why 111 Trees?

With a stick, Sundar made three lines on the ground for the three things that came to his mind: Daughter, Water, Trees.

And the magic number 111 stayed with him.

But when he proposed to the villagers that the birth of every girl child be celebrated with the planting of 111 trees, they protested. Sundar's idea was baffling to them. Honoring girls went against age-old customs and beliefs.

What Is Gender Inequality?

Gender inequality is when one gender is favored over another by individuals, families and communities. In India, all studies show that gender inequality has been part of everyday life for centuries. India was originally an agricultural, or farming, society, where an extra pair of male hands was valued in the fields, so the birth of a boy was a cause for celebration. A girl, however, was considered a disappointment and a burden. For a girl, families had to come up with money for a dowry (money given to the groom's family), and they often could not afford to give a daughter an education.

This gender bias, formed centuries ago, continued into modern times and crept into all walks of life in India.

Sundar learned that Rajasthan had a shameful record of not taking care of its girls. Many died at birth or after because of neglect and malnutrition, and many others didn't have the chance to be born at all. With new advances in science, parents were able to find out the sex of their unborn child. If the child was a girl, they often chose not to go ahead with the pregnancy.

Sundar's Plan

Despite the villagers' protests, Sundar was not one to give up. He proposed that when a girl was born, villagers donate 21 000 Indian rupees ($295 USD), and the family of the girl donate 10 000 Indian rupees ($140 USD). This money would be invested for eighteen years, after which it could be used for the girl's education or wedding expenses.

In some Indian villages, girls as young as ten are given away in marriage. Sundar wanted to put an end to this cruel practice. He asked the family of every girl born in Piplantri to sign papers promising to send their daughter to school and not marry her off before the legal age of eighteen.

The family and the entire community also had to ensure that the 111 trees remained healthy and grew along with the girl.

The girls and women of Piplantri tie prayers and sacred threads to the trees.

Aloe vera grows in abundance.

Aloe Vera

To keep the trees healthy, the villagers planted aloe vera plants, a natural termite repellent, around them. The aloe vera grew in abundance — and the women saw a business opportunity. They turned the plants into health products to sell.

For the first time, the women of Piplantri have a way to earn a livelihood.

The tall trees of Piplantri

Extraordinary Change

Today, more than a quarter of a million trees cover Piplantri. The once barren land has become fertile. The birds and other animals have returned. Brick houses have replaced mud homes. The roads are paved and clean and have streetlights.

People of India still struggle to protect their environment, and it might be a long time before everyone welcomes the birth of little girls and boys with equal delight — but the story of Piplantri is triggering a change. The government of India honored Piplantri with the President's Award in 2007 and declared it a model village.

Shyam Sundar Paliwal is a pioneer and continues to be an activist and ally in the field of eco-feminism, a movement that connects feminism — the belief that women and men should have equal rights and opportunities — to the environment. He believes there is a sacred connection between Daughter, Water and Trees. When the bond between them is strengthened, extraordinary change can take place.

Like it did in Piplantri.

How Did Sundar Become an Eco-Feminist?

Sundar lost his mother at a very young age, and his father raised him to respect all living things. When Sundar's daughters were born, he could not understand why the people he knew preferred boys to girls.

It was when he lost his own daughter that he decided to encourage a new way of thinking.

A desert transformed into a forest

Are You an Eco-Feminist?

Do you care about the environment?
Do you want to become eco-friendlier?
Do you want boys and girls to be treated equally?
Do you think that all living things should be treated with respect and dignity?

If you answered yes to these questions, you are already an eco-feminist!
Now it's time to take action! Find out more about organizations that fight to
protect the environment and promote equality for girls:

Plan International is a member of a global organization dedicated to advancing
children's rights and equality for girls. Visit plan-international.org/because-i-am-a-girl
and read about their Because I am a Girl campaign.

Girls Not Brides is a global partnership committed to ending child marriage
and enabling girls to fulfill their potential. Visit girlsnotbrides.org.

One Tree Planted is an environmental charity dedicated to making it easier for
individuals and businesses to help give back to the environment and create a
healthier climate. All by planting trees! Visit onetreeplanted.org.

Tree Canada has helped plant more than 82 million trees in Canada and is
dedicated to improving the lives of Canadians by planting and nurturing trees
while teaching about the value of trees. Visit treecanada.ca.

Get involved!